OCEAN
LIFE CONNECTIONS

By Raymond Bergin

BEARPORT
PUBLISHING

Minneapolis, Minnesota

Credits

Cover and title page, © by YamMo/Getty Images, © marrio31/iStock, © MartinLisner/iStock, © Milan__Jovic/iStock, © Yann-HUBERT/iStock, © scubaluna/iStock, and © TOSHIHARU ARAKAWA/iStock; 4–5, © Georgette Douwma/Getty Images; 6–7, © Andrew/AdobeStock; 8–9, © Magnus Larsson/iStock; 10–11, © WhitcombeRD/Getty Images; 13, © armiblue/iStock; 14–15, © narvikk/iStock; 16–17, © roclwyr/Getty Images; 18–19, © Reinhard Dirscherl/Alamy; 20–21, © Christopher Kimmel/Getty Images; 23, © luoman/iStock; 24, © Olga Mazyarkina/iStock; 24–25, © Olaf Doering/Alamy; 26–27, © by YamMo/Getty Images; 27, © All Canada Photos/Alamy; 28, © atese/iStock; 29 step 1, © Zuraisham Salleh/iStock; 29 step 2, © Daisy-Daisy/iStock; 29 step 3, © SolStock/iStock; 29 step 4, © monkeybusinessimages/iStock; and 29 step 5, © Love the wind/Shutterstock.

Bearport Publishing Company Product Development Team

President: Jen Jenson; Director of Product Development: Spencer Brinker; Senior Editor: Allison Juda; Editor: Charly Haley; Associate Editor: Naomi Reich; Senior Designer: Colin O'Dea; Associate Designer: Elena Klinkner; Associate Designer: Kayla Eggert; Product Development Assistant: Anita Stasson

Library of Congress Cataloging-in-Publication Data

Names: Bergin, Raymond, 1968- author.
Title: Ocean life connections / by Raymond Bergin.
Description: Minneapolis, Minnesota : Bearport Publishing Company, [2023] | Series: Life on earth! Biodiversity explained | Includes bibliographical references and index.
Identifiers: LCCN 2022033674 (print) | LCCN 2022033675 (ebook) | ISBN 9798885094085 (library binding) | ISBN 9798885095303 (paperback) | ISBN 9798885096454 (ebook)
Subjects: LCSH: Marine biodiversity--Juvenile literature.
Classification: LCC QH91.8.B6 B47 2023 (print) | LCC QH91.8.B6 (ebook) | DDC 578.77--dc23/eng/20220826
LC record available at https://lccn.loc.gov/2022033674
LC ebook record available at https://lccn.loc.gov/2022033675

For more information, write to Bearport Publishing, 5357 Penn Avenue South, Minneapolis, MN 55419.

Contents

A Connected World

Tiny plankton float through the ocean. Thin outer shells have kept them safe for hundreds of millions of years—but not anymore. The plankton are losing their protective coverings and dying off. So, the shrimp, snails, and jellyfish that eat plankton go hungry. Then, the fish and larger ocean animals that feed on those sea creatures don't have as much food. The loss of such small ocean life has a huge effect. What's happening to life on Earth?

The largest animal on Earth eats one of the oceans' tiniest living things. A blue whale eats tons of krill every day. Krill feed on plankton (*above*).

A Planet Full of Life

Earth is covered in many **biomes**—areas of land and sea where the **climate** and natural features are a perfect fit for certain kinds of plants and animals. Wetlands, tundras, grasslands, deserts, forests, and oceans are all biomes.

Every biome is home to a connected community of life. This wide variety of connected life is called **biodiversity**. Each ocean biome can include everything from microscopic plankton to massive kelp plants taller than a 17-story building.

There may be as many as 10 million **species** of plants and animals living in different ocean biomes. Much of this life has yet to be discovered. Each year, scientists identify about 2,000 new species.

In healthy ocean biomes, kelp plants grow in forests under the water.

It All Fits Together

Each living thing is important for the survival of the rest. The animals and plants within biomes rely on one another for food, shelter, and protection. Shrimp build burrows that also provide homes for fish. Barnacles attach themselves to whales for protection. Even after death, organisms are important. They sink to the ocean floor and feed deep-sea creatures.

Some sea creatures are in **symbiotic** relationships. They help each other. Clown fish hide from enemies among the stinging tentacles of sea anemones. In return, clown fish give anemones food—their own fishy poop!

When these life connections are disrupted, ocean biomes become weaker. Fewer plants and animals perform important roles for their neighbors, forcing others to relocate or risk their own survival in an ever-changing biome.

Death at Sea

Healthy oceans are rich in biodiversity. But the oceans are no longer healthy, and it's mostly because of people. The way we live is heating up the planet and causing the climate to change. This is impacting ocean biomes around the world.

At the same time, the survival of some fish populations is threatened by overfishing. Pollution is ending up in the waters. And we pave over some waterways to build homes and businesses along the coast. All of this is killing ocean life and has wide-reaching consequences.

A third of ocean **mammals**, sharks, and coral reefs are in danger of **extinction** due to harm from humans. It is estimated that more than half of the world's ocean species could die by 2100.

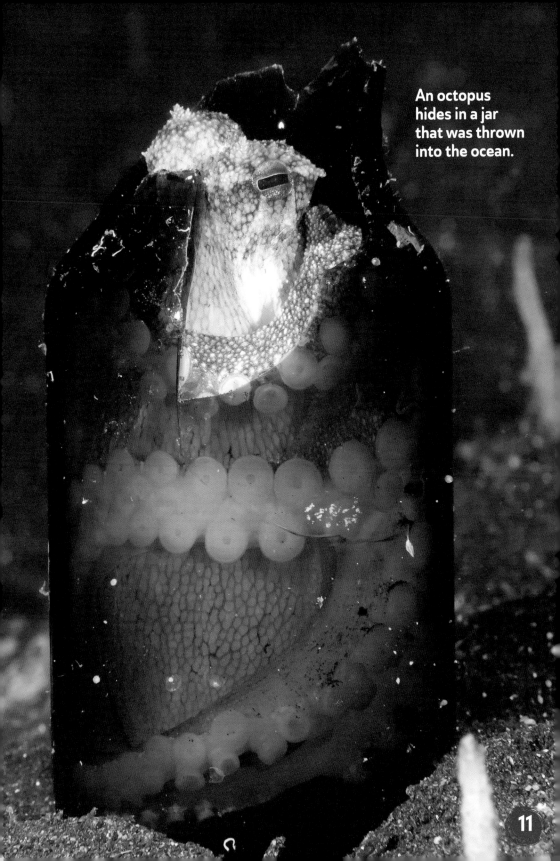

An octopus hides in a jar that was thrown into the ocean.

Crumbling Coral

Coral reefs are home to countless sea creatures that use them as places to make homes, find food, reproduce, and raise their young. However, these living structures are being threatened. Oceans take in much of the extra **carbon dioxide** that goes into the air when we burn fuel. The more carbon absorbed by an ocean, the more **acidic** its waters become. The increased acidity makes coral weak. Some coral has even died. Without healthy coral, millions of creatures lose food, shelter, and even their lives.

The coral reefs off the coast of the Northwestern Hawaiian Islands support more than 7,000 species of plants and animals. As is the case with other reefs, this coral is at risk due to acidification.

Reefs are made from the skeletons of tiny animals called coral polyps.

Melting Homes

Earth's oceans take in carbon dioxide and prevent air pollution from staying around the planet. But we are making more pollution than the water can absorb. The extra gases are trapping heat around Earth and are raising both air and water temperatures.

Heat is destroying another important part of Earth's ocean biomes. Like reefs, glaciers and ice sheets provide some animals places to hunt, find shelter, and raise their young. As the ice melts, polar animals are forced onto land. There, they must eat different food, find new shelter, and learn how to live in unfamiliar territory.

Plants and other food found on land are harder for polar bears to chew and digest. The bears are also forced to compete with grizzlies for the limited food options.

Polar bears used to hunt seals on ice. Now, there are fewer pieces of sea ice and fewer seals.

Kelp Needs Help!

Some of the species hurt by rising water temperatures are creatures that have a big impact on their biome. These **keystone** species are crucial to the health of their whole habitat.

When sea stars living in Californian kelp forests began dying, life within the long strips of seaweed nearly collapsed. Sea stars ate sea urchins. So, when they died off, the sea urchin population exploded. The urchins, in turn, ate so much kelp that the plants couldn't grow into large forests. Soon, kelp forests disappeared, along with the creatures that lived, ate, and **spawned** there.

Sea otters helped bring California's underwater forests back. The furry creatures also eat the sea urchins that would otherwise munch away all of the kelp.

Turtle Trap

Sometimes, humans more directly harm keystone creatures. Shrimp boats use huge nets to gather their catch. Unfortunately, they also unintentionally scoop up sea turtles, many of which die when they can't make it to the surface to breathe.

Sea turtles are incredibly important to their habitat. They keep the number of jellyfish low and eat sponges that crowd out coral reefs. Their eggshells and poop **fertilize** coastal plants. Turtle eggs are also a tasty snack for birds and fish.

Shrimp nets accidentally catch fish, dolphins, and even whales. For every pound (0.5 kg) of shrimp caught, as many as 10 lb (5 kg) of unwanted sea life ends up in fishing nets.

Where the City Meets the Sea

Harm to oceans can also come from what happens on dry lands that used to be wet and full of sea life. Many of the world's largest cities were built on **estuaries**, places where rivers meet the sea.

Almost 40 percent of estuaries in the United States have been drained and filled in. People construct buildings and roads where water once was.

Estuaries are often called the oceans' nurseries because they shelter young fish, oysters, and crabs. When these places are destroyed by humans, young creatures die before growing up. They have no chance to make their own babies and **replenish** their populations.

Trashing the Oceans

When estuaries are destroyed and replaced by coastal homes, hotels, and restaurants, a lot of the trash people produce in these places ends up in the oceans. Plastic litter often looks like food to birds, sea turtles, and fish. But when they eat it, they can get sick or die from the **toxins** in the plastic. Ocean plastic gets broken down into pieces so small that even plankton can eat it. Then, these tiny creatures with plastic in their stomachs are eaten by larger animals. The plastic makes its way through the food web—all the way back to humans.

A floating pile of trash twice the size of Texas was nicknamed the Great Pacific Garbage Patch. It stretches from the West Coast of North America all the way to East Asia!

Most of the Great Pacific Garbage Patch is plastic.

People and the Oceans

Clearly problems in the oceans don't stay below the waves. When ocean life becomes unhealthy, so does our life on land.

Oceans produce half of the oxygen we breathe. They also remove a third of the carbon dioxide we pump into the air. These large bodies of water give us cleaner air while also reducing global warming. Every day, more than 3 billion people turn to the oceans for food, too. If we want the oceans to keep caring for us, we must care for them.

The oceans are also an important source of our medicine. Ingredients made from sea plants and animals are turned into drugs that treat cancer, infections, and even COVID.

Ocean Life Returns

All over the world, people are beginning to recognize how important the wide variety of ocean life is to the health of the entire planet. Estuaries are being restored. There is less development along the coasts, and people are joining in shore cleanups. New rules are designed to stop fishing practices that catch the wrong kind of fish in huge nets. These small steps are starting to help.

The oceans feed us. They give us air to breathe and help keep our planet cool. We owe our lives to the life connections found in our oceans.

One organization cleaning up the Great Pacific Garbage Patch has removed almost 240,000 lb (110,000 kg) of trash from the water. They have found fishing gear, shoes, laundry baskets, and even toilets!

Save the Oceans

What can we do to save the wide open oceans? If we keep the seas and coastlines clean and reduce the amount of heat-trapping carbon dioxide we make, we can take a step in the right direction.

Say no to single-use items such as bags, straws, and water bottles. Instead, choose reusable items.

Always place your trash into secure garbage containers or recycling bins when boating or near the shore.

Take part in beach cleanup days and coastal habitat restoration projects if you live near the water.

If it is possible and safe, walk, ride a bike, or take public transportation to get where you're going instead of releasing carbon dioxide into the air with a car.

Electricity is often made by burning fuel. Save electricity by turning off lights and unplugging electronics when you're not using them.

Glossary

acidic containing a chemical that has a very sharp or sour taste

biodiversity the existence of many different kinds of plants and animals in an environment

biomes regions with a particular climate and environment where certain kinds of plants and animals live

carbon dioxide a gas given off when fossil fuels are burned

climate the typical weather in a place

estuaries the places where ocean tides meet river currents

extinction when a type of animal or plant dies out completely

fertilize to add nutrients to soil that make it easier for plants and trees to grow

keystone a plant or animal that is crucial to the success of its ecosystem

mammals warm-blooded animals that have hair and drink milk from their mothers as babies

replenish to fill or build back up again

spawned produced or released a lot of eggs

species groups that animals and plants are divided into according to similar characteristics

symbiotic relating to a relationship between two different kinds of living things in which each gives to the other something that helps it thrive

toxins poisons

Read More

Bergin, Raymond. *Melting Ice (What on Earth? Climate Change Explained).* Minneapolis: Bearport Publishing, 2022.

Finan, Catherine C. *The Oceans (X-Treme Facts: Science).* Minneapolis: Bearport Publishing, 2021.

French, Jess. *Earth's Incredible Oceans.* New York: DK Publishing, 2021.

Hamby, Rachel. *Saving the Oceans from Plastic (Saving Earth's Biomes).* Lake Elmo, MN: Focus Readers, 2020.

Learn More Online

1. Go to **www.factsurfer.com** or scan the QR code below.

2. Enter "**Ocean Connections**" into the search box.

3. Click on the cover of this book to see a list of websites.

Index

About the Author

Raymond Bergin lives less than an hour from the Atlantic coast. Whenever he gets the chance, he likes to walk barefoot along the beach. He always brings a few garbage bags with him to pick up any trash he finds along the way.